★ ★ ☆

James Buchanan

James Buchanan

Allison Lassieur

AMERICA'S
15TH
PRESIDENT

Children's Press®
A Division of Scholastic Inc.
New York / Toronto / London / Auckland / Sydney
Mexico City / New Delhi / Hong Kong
Danbury, Connecticut

J
B
Buchanan, J.

Library of Congress Cataloging-in-Publication Data

Lassieur, Allison.
    James Buchanan / by Allison Lassieur
        p. cm. — (Encyclopedia of presidents. Second series)
        Summary: A biography of the fifteenth president of the United States, with
information about his childhood, family, political career, presidency, and legacy.
Includes bibliographical references and index.
    ISBN 0-516-22884-6
    1. Buchanan, James, 1791–1868—Juvenile literature. 2. Presidents—United
States—Biography—Juvenile literature. [1. Buchanan, James, 1791–1868.
2. Presidents.] I. Title. II. Series.
E437.L37 2003
973.6'8'092—dc22   2003015936

CHILDREN'S PRESS and associated logos are trademarks and or registered
trademarks of Scholastic Library Publishing. SCHOLASTIC and associated
logos are trademarks and or registered trademarks of Scholastic Inc.
1 2 3 4 5 6 7 8 9 10 R 13 12 11 10 09 08 07 06 05 04

Contents

Chapter 1

Immigrant's Son

When future president James Buchanan was born in 1791, the United States was a place of excitement and opportunity. Ten years earlier, the country had gained its independence from Great Britain. Only two years earlier, George Washington had been elected the first president under the new U.S. Constitution. Philadelphia, Boston, and New York were bustling cities. Plans were being made to build a new national capital on land in the District of Columbia along the Potomac River.

The new country was beginning to attract new immigrants. One of these was James Buchanan's father, also named James. A native of County Donegal in Ireland, James Buchanan Senior arrived in the summer of 1783. He was 22 years old, and he came at the invitation of his uncle, Joshua Russell, who owned a tavern near Gettysburg, Pennsylvania. James started out working for his uncle.

Soon James Senior went to work for John Tom, who ran a tavern and trading post in Cove Gap, Pennsylvania. Tom needed an assistant to help manage his growing business. In 1787 James bought the trading post, which included several log cabins, barns and stables, a storehouse and store building, fields, and an orchard. He named the property Stony Batter. In only a few years, James Buchanan Senior had become a successful businessman and landowner.

In 1788, James married Elizabeth Speer. He was 27 years old and she was 21. They began their married life in a log cabin on the Stony Batter property. In 1789, the couple had their first child, a daughter named Mary. Then, on April 23, 1791, Elizabeth gave birth to a son. The proud parents named him James Buchanan, after his father. Not long after young James was born, his sister Mary died. The family continued to grow, however. By the time he was 11, James had four sisters—Jane, Maria, Sarah, and Harriet. Four brothers were born later, two of them after James left home.

James Senior continued his success in business. He bought a 300-acre (120-hectare) farm called Dunwoodie, in the nearby town of Mercersburg. When young James was six, the Buchanans moved to a spacious two-story home in Mercersburg. The small town was surrounded by rolling green hills and shadowy oak groves where a growing boy could explore. For the first time, he had playmates other than his sisters. He started school at the Old Stone Academy. As at

This log cabin, now at Mercersburg Academy, was moved from Stony Batter. James Buchanan identified this cabin as the one in which he was born in 1791.

other schools of the time, James and his classmates were soon learning to read Latin as well as English.

James's early years at Stony Batter and in Mercersburg gave him a lasting love for the countryside and the slow pace of village life. He spent most of his adult years in bustling cities, but he always looked forward to returning to the quiet of a country farm. James was also influenced by following his father's business affairs. He learned the importance of keeping good records, and trained himself to have good handwriting. He kept detailed records of his own activities and expenses throughout his life.

Like many boys, James did not always get along with his father. His father would sometimes give him jobs too difficult for him to complete and then would criticize him when they weren't done properly. James rarely received praise from his father, no matter how well he did. He loved and respected his father, but longed for his approval.

His mother Elizabeth was more affectionate. She taught him the elements of her deeply held Presbyterian faith. He also learned from her to deal with misfortunes calmly and methodically. Later in life he said, "I attribute any little distinction which I may have acquired in the world to the blessing which He conferred upon me in granting me such a mother."

As James approached the end of his schooling at the academy, he and his parents began to discuss his further education. His mother wanted him to become a minister. His father suggested that a career in law might be more suitable. As the oldest son in a large family, James might one day need to help provide for his sisters and brothers, which would be difficult on a minister's income. At the recommendation of a family friend, Dr. John King, James enrolled at Dickinson College in Carlisle, Pennsylvania, about 50 miles (80 kilometers) east of Mercersburg. He was 16 years old.

Turbulent College Days

When James enrolled at Dickinson in 1807, the college was going through a difficult period. The students were unsupervised and disorderly, often getting into drunken brawls in the town of Carlisle. James later wrote, "The college was in wretched condition; and I have often since regretted that I had not been sent to some other institution. There was no efficient discipline, and the young men did pretty much as they pleased."

At first he studied hard and obeyed all the rules, but this won him few friends. "To be a sober, plodding, industrious youth was to incur the ridicule of the mass of the students," he recalled later. He began to join the other students in breaking the rules and defying their teachers, but he continued to be a good student.

Then one beautiful September morning in 1808, a messenger delivered a letter to the Buchanan home. James's father read it, then gave it to James and left the room. James had been expelled from school due to bad behavior! James's father was disappointed, and James was "mortified to the soul," as he later recalled. Dr. King agreed to help James be reinstated, but gave James a stern lecture and made him promise to change his ways. When he was readmitted, James

Old West Hall at Dickinson College as it looked when James Buchanan was a student from 1807 to 1809.

focused on his studies and made excellent grades. In the spring, he was accepted

for graduation.

Each year the school awarded senior honors to two students. James was

nominated, and his grades qualified him for honors, but the faculty refused to

consider him. He still had a reputation as a troublemaker, and he had shown little

respect for his teachers. James was furious, and some of his classmates and teach-

ers supported him. His father, on the other hand, urged James to accept the decision like a man. Before graduation day, the school leaders compromised. They allowed James to give a speech at graduation ceremonies but still refused to award him honors.

"I left college . . . feeling but little attachment towards the Alma Mater [Dickinson College]," Buchanan later wrote. Still, the experience helped him learn to deal with setbacks in a mature way. Late in his life, he gave up his resentment of Dickinson College and supported its plans for growth and improvement.

An Ambitious Young Lawyer

When James Buchanan graduated from college, he was 18 years old and ready to study law. At the time, an aspiring lawyer studied the law with an experienced lawyer who served as a preceptor, or tutor. Buchanan applied to study with a respected lawyer in Lancaster, Pennsylvania, named James Hopkins, an acquaintance of his father. He was accepted, and in December 1809, Buchanan arrived in Lancaster to begin the next phase of his education.

At the time, Lancaster was one of the largest towns in the United States. Only New York City and Philadelphia had larger populations than Lancaster County. The turnpike road from Philadelphia to Lancaster was one of the best roads in America. The Conestoga Creek flowed near the town. The huge freight

An early sketch of Penn Square in Lancaster, Pennsylvania, where Buchanan studied and practiced law.

wagons that traveled the turnpike took the creek's name and became known as Conestoga wagons.

After the trouble he had gotten into during college, Buchanan was determined to succeed in his law studies. Years later he wrote that "I can say, with truth, that I have never known a harder student than I was at that period in my life." He read legal books and documents all day. Then in the early evening, he would take long walks, thinking about everything he had read and repeating it to himself out loud.

Conestoga Wagons Transform American Life

When James Buchanan arrived in Lancaster, railroads played no part in the transportation system. Wherever possible, people traveled and transported goods by water, using the sea and large rivers as their highways. Inland, they relied on dirt or gravel roads, hauling goods on wagons drawn by horses, mules, or oxen.

Conestoga wagons first appeared in Pennsylvania in the 1700s. Farmers used them to carry heavy loads long distances. One large wagon pulled by six horses could carry loads of up to eight tons. Freight carriers organized wagon trains (long caravans of Conestogas) to move goods along the roads.

A graceful Conestoga wagon.

The Conestoga wagon was graceful as well as practical. The curved bottom of the wagon box rose at both ends, resembling a boat. This design kept cargo from shifting when the wagon went up and down steep hills. The white fabric top, which kept out sun, dust, and rain, was curved in the same way. The wagons came to be known as "ships of inland commerce."

☆ ☆ ☆

By 1812 Buchanan's studies were almost over, and he would soon qualify to practice as a lawyer. Again, he faced a decision: Where should he practice? He could return to Mercersburg, where his family still lived, or travel to Philadelphia, the state's largest city. In the end, he decided to stay in Lancaster. He found a small office and put notices in newspapers advertising his new law practice. He also was appointed deputy prosecutor for Lancaster County. The small fees he earned as a part-time prosecutor would help pay his bills until he could build up his law practice.

The Lawyer Turns to Politics

Buchanan began by drawing up wills, leases, and other routine legal papers for clients. More experienced lawyers referred small cases to him. In the first year, his income was $938.

At the same time, he began attending meetings of the local Federalist party. Once a powerful force in the national government, the Federalists had lost much of their influence in Washington, but they were still powerful in Pennsylvania and other northern states. In 1814, the Federalists were angrily opposed to the War of 1812, which the United States was fighting against Great Britain. The war had brought trade with Britain to a standstill, injuring the traders and merchants who belonged to the Federalist party. Young Buchanan gave speeches in Lancaster against the war. In August 1814, the Federalists nominated Buchanan to run for a seat in the state legislature.

On the very day he was nominated, however, a British armed force captured Washington, D.C., and burned public buildings, including the Capitol and the White House. News of the attack reached Lancaster the next day. Even though Buchanan was against the war, he knew that a political candidate with military experience was more likely to win an election. He signed up to fight, and two days later, he was on his way to Baltimore with a troop of volunteers who called themselves the Lancaster County Dragoons. His life as a soldier was brief. When the dragoons arrived in Baltimore, an officer ordered them to requisition some horses for army use. They rounded up the horses and presented them to the officer

Fast Facts

THE WAR OF 1812

Who: The United States against Great Britain.

When: The U.S. declared war in June 1812. The war was ended by the Treaty of Ghent, signed in December 1814, but fighting continued into January 1815.

Why: Britain was restricting U.S. shipping, seizing cargoes and sailors from U.S. ships. It was also interfering with settlement in U.S. western territories and providing help to Native Americans who were attacking American settlers.

Where: In the United States, Canada, and on the Atlantic Ocean. The U.S. organized several unsuccessful invasions of Canada while surrendering forts in the Northwest. In 1813, the U.S. navy defeated a British fleet in Lake Erie, leading to land victories at Detroit and at the Thames River (in nearby Ontario). In 1814, British captured Washington, D.C., and burned public buildings, but were defeated soon afterward in Baltimore. British troops threatened New Orleans but were driven off in January 1815 by a force led by Andrew Jackson.

Outcome: In the Treaty of Ghent (signed December 24, 1814), both sides agreed to boundaries set up before the war. Britain agreed to end impressment of American seamen and give up British forts south of the Great Lakes. The treaty also settled disputes about fishing rights and commercial relations.

British troops set fire to the White House and other government buildings in Washington in August 1814.

with a flourish. Within days, however, the British were defeated in battle in the Baltimore harbor and sailed away. The dragoons were honorably discharged, and they returned to Lancaster.

Buchanan returned home from military duty just in time to campaign for his election. The Federalists were popular in Lancaster, and Buchanan won. A few weeks later, he boarded the stagecoach and headed to Harrisburg, Pennsylvania's new state capital, to start his political career as state assemblyman.

Learning the Ropes in State Politics

The state legislature met for only a few months during the year. Buchanan arrived in Harrisburg expecting that sessions of the state legislature would be filled with excitement and interest. He soon learned that he had little to do. He presented a few local petitions and voted on bills proposed by more experienced legislators.

Eager to make a name for himself, Buchanan decided to give a speech. In early 1815, the legislature was debating on how to raise enough people for the local militia. Some legislators wanted a conscription plan, in which men would be drafted into service. Others backed a volunteer army, in which soldiers signed up to fight. On February 1, 1815, Buchanan made an emotional speech in favor of the volunteer plan. It was an excellent speech, but Buchanan soon learned that nearly all of his fellow Federalists favored the conscription plan! His own party members spoke against him, and members of the opposing Democratic-Republican party laughingly urged him to leave the Federalists and join them. Buchanan was mortified. He resolved to be much more careful in the future, and he kept quiet for the rest of his term.

He worried that resentment against his speech would keep him from being reelected, but decided to run again anyway. On the Fourth of July, he delivered a holiday address to the citizens of Lancaster. He blasted the Democratic party and promoted Federalist ideas. The speech was a grand success, and soon afterward the Federalists nominated him for reelection. He won a second one-year term. Since assemblymen traditionally served only two terms, he then returned to Lancaster and threw his full energy into his law practice.

A Reputation for Good Work —————————

Over the next four years, Buchanan built his practice into one of the most respected legal offices in Lancaster. He took a variety of work, including civil and criminal suits, tax work, settling estates, and serving notices. He was so detail oriented that some people called him a "hair splitter."

One difficult case strengthened his reputation as a courtroom attorney. A Federalist judge, Walter Franklin, was being *impeached*—charged with serious offenses that could cause his removal from office. Buchanan agreed to defend him and succeeded in gaining the judge's acquittal. The case brought him respect among lawyers and attracted more clients. Between 1816 and 1818, his yearly income jumped from $3,200 to nearly $8,000. Still in his twenties, he was becoming a prosperous young man.

Love, Scandal, and Heartbreak —————————

When Buchanan returned to Lancaster in 1816, he began to attend parties and society balls, where he attracted the attention of young ladies from prominent families. One of these was Ann Coleman, whom he met in 1818. She was the daughter of one of Lancaster's richest men, Robert Coleman, an Irish immigrant who had made his fortune in the iron industry. Coleman was a hot-tempered man who was determined that his daughter would marry well.

Ann was a striking young woman, 22 years old, with black hair and dark eyes. She was proud and strong-willed. Buchanan began courting her, and in the summer of 1819 he proposed marriage. She happily said yes. However, her family disapproved of the match. They suggested that Buchanan only wanted to marry Ann for her family's money. When he was away for long periods on business, they suggested that he did not really care for her. Ann began to wonder. That fall, on his way home from a business trip, Buchanan casually visited an old family friend. By coincidence, a pretty young lady named Grace Hubley came to visit at the same time. Gossips soon told Ann that her fiancé was keeping company with another woman. Angry and jealous, she broke off the engagement.

A few days later, on December 4, Ann traveled to Philadelphia with her younger sister Sarah. During her stay, she became desperately ill one night and died before morning. Buchanan received the news soon afterward. According to one report, Ann had a fit of hysterics over the broken engagement, went into convulsions, and died.

Buchanan was crushed by grief and guilt. He immediately wrote to Mr. Coleman. "You have lost a child . . . I have lost the only earthly object of my affections. . . . I feel that my happiness will be buried with her in the grave," he wrote. He pleaded to be allowed to visit the Coleman house, where Ann's body

A portrait of Ann Coleman, to whom Buchanan was engaged.

was on view. Ann's father returned the letter unopened and unread. Buchanan was not allowed to pay his last respects or to attend the funeral. Buchanan shut himself in his rooms and refused to come out for days. Finally, he emerged and went back to Mercersburg to spend Christmas with his family. He did not return to Lancaster until after the New Year.

Buchanan Flees to Politics

Buchanan returned to a difficult situation in early 1820. Ann Coleman's death was still the talk of Lancaster gossips, and he was still grieving. To distract himself, Buchanan worked harder than ever at his law practice.

That spring, he announced that he would run for the U.S. House of Representatives in the fall election. He spent the summer campaigning. His opponents continued to mention Ann Coleman's death, yet he learned to ignore their abuse. He made few campaign speeches, leaving most of the campaigning to the strong and active Federalist party in the region. In the fall, he was elected to the House of Representatives.

In the summer of 1821, before he left for Washington, Buchanan was struck by another blow. His father was killed by a fall from a wagon. Buchanan discovered that his father had left no will. He spent the summer untangling his father's estate so that his mother and his younger sisters and brothers would be cared for. Finally, in November 1821, Buchanan boarded a stagecoach for Washington to attend the first session of the new congress, leaving the sad memories of Ann and the death of his father behind.

Chapter 2

Mr. Buchanan Goes to Washington

Rebuilding in the Capital ————————

When James Buchanan arrived in 1821, Washington, D.C., was still a small town, with fewer residents than Lancaster County. Major government buildings burned by the British in 1814 were still being repaired, and cows still grazed on the hill leading up to the Capitol, where the House of Representatives met.

Politics in the capital city were being reformed and rebuilt, too. Democratic-Republicans had won every presidential election since 1800, and Buchanan's party, the Federalists, was shrinking in power and influence. In fact, Democratic-Republican James Monroe was reelected in 1820 with 231 out of 232 electoral votes. One newspaper welcomed an "Era of Good Feeling" because there was so little political competition between the parties. As a Federalist congressman, Buchanan was part of a small minority, but he went to work getting acquainted with other congressmen and studying the issues the Congress was considering.

Bankruptcy and Local Improvements ————

In his first years in Congress, Buchanan gained recognition for his views on several issues. One was the bankruptcy bill. At that time, only businesses could declare bankruptcy. If the business ran out of money and could not pay its debts, it could file for bankruptcy, which would allow it to continue operating while trying to raise money to pay the money it owed. A court helped supervise its operations and could allow the business to pay only a part of what it owed.

Now a new bankruptcy bill proposed to let individuals, including farmers, craftsmen, and laborers, gain protection under bankruptcy laws. Up to this time, individuals who fell into debt could be thrown into jail until they repaid all their debts. Bankruptcy protection would allow them to continue working while a court decided how much of their debt they would be required to pay. The bill was popular with many congressmen since it seemed to give individuals the same protections as large businesses. At first, Buchanan supported it.

The bankruptcy bill was not popular with merchants, however. If individuals could declare bankruptcy, they could get away without paying for goods or services, and the merchants would lose that money. Many prosperous merchants in the northeast were still supporters of the Federalist party. After further study, Buchanan changed his mind about the bankruptcy bill and announced that he was opposed to it.

In a long speech to the House, Buchanan warned that the bankruptcy bill would allow the government to take property (the money individuals owed) away from legitimate businesses. He feared that individuals would take advantage of the law to get around paying their bills. The bankruptcy bill "would be a perfect

The United States Capitol, at the top of Capitol Hill, as it appeared when James Buchanan arrived in Washington.

monster in this country," he said, "where our institutions depend altogether upon the virtue of the people." Government and society are organized to protect property rights, he said, and the bankruptcy law would limit those rights. His arguments helped defeat the bill.

A second issue Buchanan tackled was a bill that would allow the federal government to collect tolls on the Cumberland Road to provide money for repairs. At first he voted for the bill because some of the money would go to maintain the part of the road in Pennsylvania. President Monroe vetoed the bill, however, explaining that he believed it was unconstitutional. Like many Democratic-Republicans, he believed the Constitution did not allow the federal government to collect money for local improvements. He said that state or local governments had the right and the responsibility to collect money for improvements in their own territory.

Most Federalists were in favor of using federal funds to help build and repair roads, canals, and other improvements that would benefit trade. Even so, Buchanan was impressed by President Monroe's arguments. As a student of the Constitution, he concluded that Monroe was correct to protect the rights of individual states against the powers of the federal government. Buchanan broke with the Federalist party on the issue and continued to oppose federal support for local improvements throughout his career.

The Election of 1824

As 1824 approached, it was clear that the presidential election would mark a new beginning in American politics. For nearly 24 years, one party, the Democratic-Republicans, had been in power. Many voters, especially in the rapidly growing states west of the Appalachian Mountains, believed it was time for a change. Since the Federalist party was no longer strong enough to run a strong candidate, the Democratic-Republican party began breaking apart into factions, some of which would become new parties in the future.

In earlier years, candidates for president were nominated by a congressional *caucus* made up of a party's congressmen and senators. In 1824, the Democratic-Republican congressional caucus chose William Crawford from Georgia, who was serving as President Monroe's secretary of the treasury. Many in other regions were unhappy with this choice, and they nominated their own candidates. In Massachusetts, the state legislature nominated John Quincy Adams, Monroe's secretary of state. Kentucky nominated its favorite son, Henry Clay, and Tennessee nominated the military hero of the War of 1812, Andrew Jackson. With four strong candidates, all from the same party, this would be a presidential election like none before it.

Which of the four would James Buchanan support? As a northeasterner, he might be expected to support John Quincy Adams. As a supporter of states' rights and limited national government, he might support Crawford. As a supporter of protecting business, he could have favored Clay. Instead, he threw his support to Andrew Jackson, the rough-and-tumble general from Tennessee. Jackson was an outsider who had spent little time in Washington. He had a wild, unruly appearance and rough manners. Yet he had a strong aura of leadership and great appeal to voters. He promised to take the government out of the hands of cultivated eastern politicians and return it to "the people." Jackson seemed an odd choice for Buchanan to make, but he stuck with it.

The campaign soon became ugly and negative. Clay was accused of being a gambler. Jackson was accused of being a murderer (he once killed a man in a duel). John Quincy Adams was accused of not being "American" enough. He had served for many years as a U.S. diplomat in Europe, and his wife was British.

On election day, there was no clear winner. Andrew Jackson had the most popular votes and the most electoral votes. Because no candidate had a majority of the electoral votes, however, the election would be decided by the House of Representatives. Washington swarmed with politicians trying to persuade congressmen to vote for their candidate. Jackson supporters argued that the House should elect their man because he had the most popular and electoral votes. There were rumors that if Adams would throw his support to Jackson, Jackson would

General Andrew Jackson, known to his soldiers as "Old Hickory." Buchanan supported him for president in 1824. Jackson was elected president in 1828 and served for eight years.

appoint Adams secretary of state. Meanwhile, the opponents of Jackson organized to deny him the presidency.

During this difficult time, Buchanan made a huge political mistake. He arranged a meeting with Andrew Jackson and asked the general if he was planning to appoint Adams as secretary of state. Jackson, who did not know Buchanan well, answered that he had not yet decided. Buchanan reported Jackson's reply to others. Jackson was angry, believing that the young congressman was meddling in affairs he did not understand. After that, Jackson and his advisers never trusted Buchanan. The misunderstanding would seriously damage Buchanan's political career.

The House met to vote on February 9, 1825. According to the rules, they could vote only for one of the top three candidates: Jackson, Adams, or Crawford. Clay had finished fourth and had been eliminated. Clay threw his support to John Quincy Adams, and Adams was elected. A few days later, Adams announced that Henry Clay would be his secretary of state. Jackson's supporters were furious. They denounced the "deal" between Adams and Clay, charging that Clay had "sold" the presidency to become secretary of state. Jackson immediately declared that he would run for president in 1828.

President John Quincy Adams, who defeated Andrew Jackson in the disputed election of 1824. Four years later, Adams lost to Jackson.

New Challenges

For the next four years, Buchanan worked hard in Congress. He wrote letters, delivered speeches, cultivated powerful friendships, and continued to sharpen his political skills. In 1826, he was elected for the last time as a Federalist. For the 1828 election he formally changed his party affiliation to the Democratic-Republican party.

The 1828 election was especially difficult for Buchanan. His enemies brought up his embarrassing role in the 1824 election controversy and misquoted his old speeches to make him look bad. They accused him of supporting slavery, and of slandering a judge's wife. Buchanan defended himself by writing articles and letters to the newspapers, and urging his friends and supporters to campaign for him. In the fall, he was reelected to the House. In the presidential election Andrew Jackson easily defeated President Adams.

Buchanan began his new term as a Democratic-Republican congressman by becoming the chairman of the House Judiciary Committee, the committee that reviews bills and provisions relating to the court system of the United States. In 1831, a South Carolina congressman introduced a proposal to revise the Judiciary Act of 1789, deleting the 25th section, which gives the U.S. Supreme Court the right to review state courts' decisions that involve constitutional issues. Congressmen who believed in states' rights believed that state courts should have full power to determine the laws of their state without review of a federal court.

Even though Buchanan was generally in favor of states' rights, in this case his sense of the law led him to oppose the bill. He gave one of the most energetic speeches of his career, defending the Judiciary Act and the right of the Supreme Court to review certain state court decisions. He said that it should be the chief goal of the government to protect individual rights. If the Supreme Court could not review state decisions, state courts could deny individual rights guaranteed by the Constitution. Every state would be left to interpret the Constitution in its own way, creating confusion and dissension. Buchanan's arguments were persuasive. The House voted 138 to 51 to support his recommendation against the bill.

An Unexpected Invitation

By 1831, Buchanan had served in the House of Representatives for nearly ten years. He was beginning to consider running for higher office. President Jackson was expected to run for a second term in 1832, and Buchanan's friends suggested that he put his name up for vice president.

Then a surprising letter arrived from President Jackson himself, offering to appoint James Buchanan the U.S. minister to Russia. Buchanan realized that Jackson was trying get rid of him. In Pennsylvania politics, Buchanan had been battling with another leader, George Dallas of Philadelphia, for control of the state party. Jackson and his advisers wanted to end the dispute. If Buchanan went to Russia, George Dallas could unify the party in Pennsylvania.

At first, Buchanan refused the invitation, but he soon reconsidered. He could see that he had little chance for the vice presidential nomination. Jackson favored Martin Van Buren, his closest adviser. The appointment to Russia would also allow Buchanan to gain experience in foreign affairs, a subject that had always interested him. Finally, he agreed to accept the appointment. He began reading books on Russian history and studying French, the language spoken at the court of the Russian czar. He would make the most of this new opportunity and let others manage politics in Washington and in Pennsylvania.

St. Petersburg

Buchanan set off for Russia in the spring of 1832. The Russian capital was then St. Petersburg, one of the world's most beautiful cities. It had been designed by Czar Peter the Great in the early 1700s with majestic broad boulevards lined with elegant homes and palaces for the families of the czar and the rich noblemen of Russia. Buchanan was amazed by its elegance and style.

He soon realized that serving as a diplomat here would be expensive. It was important for him to make a good impression. He rented a large, beautiful villa to serve as his home and headquarters. It had a courtyard, stables for six horses, a carriage and sleigh house, and living quarters for the servants. Buchanan was especially pleased with his wonderful view of the river Neva, which runs through the city. He furnished the villa with expensive furniture, sculpture, porcelain and crystal, and enough china to serve a dinner for 30 people.

The czar's huge Winter Palace was one of many imposing buildings James Buchanan saw when he arrived in St. Petersburg in 1832.

The Jackson administration instructed Buchanan to negotiate the first trade agreement between the United States and Russia. He was well equipped for the task. His study of French paid off handsomely, allowing him to speak directly with Russian diplomats and with Czar Nicholas himself. He also made good use of his orderly, lawyer-like way of thinking and his long experience in political negotiations. Even so, the negotiations went slowly. He learned that the Russian imperial court, much like Washington, was filled with hidden alliances, secret meetings, and behind-the-scenes dealing. Fortunately, he was familiar with such things and found ways to use them to his advantage.

In December 1832, the trade agreement was complete and was approved by Czar Nicholas. The U.S. Senate ratified the treaty in February 1833. The United States and Russia granted each other "most favored nation" status in each other's ports, which offered the prospect that increased trade between the two countries would benefit both.

Despite the splendor of St. Petersburg and his success as minister, Buchanan was longing to return to the United States. During his absence, his mother and his young brother George had died. He was also eager to make plans for his future in politics. When friends in Pennsylvania wrote that he might gain election to one of the state's seats in the U.S. Senate, Buchanan offered his resignation to President Jackson. It was accepted.

Czar Nicholas I, the ruler of the Russian Empire, who met with Buchanan when he was U.S. minister to Russia.

In his last meeting with Czar Nicholas, the czar paid Buchanan a handsome compliment. Nicholas said he would like another minister from the United States just like Buchanan—he said he could imagine no one better. On that cordial note Buchanan sailed for home in August 1833.

Senator Buchanan

When Buchanan returned to Lancaster, he began to look for a permanent home there. By a twist of fate, the Coleman house, where his fiancée Ann Coleman had lived, was for sale, and Buchanan bought it. It was a solid, beautiful home, and apparently Buchanan did not find it strange to live there. He also hired a young housekeeper, Esther Parker (soon known to all as Miss Hetty) to organize and run his household.

As his supporters in Pennsylvania had written, there was a vacancy for a U.S. Senate seat from Pennsylvania. In those days, senators were elected not by popular vote, but by state legislatures. Buchanan put his name up for the position, and the legislature elected him. With his new home well cared for, he left once again for Washington.

Buchanan had been away from Washington during a turbulent time. During 1832 and 1833, President Jackson and Congress had been feuding over the Bank of the United States. The bank was favored by many in Congress, because it helped to regulate local banks and control the supply of money. Jackson, on the other hand, was an enemy of the bank. He believed that it was corrupt and that it favored rich merchants and discriminated against small businesses and farmers. He eventually succeeded in driving the bank out of business.

Buchanan was lucky to be away during most of the bank battle. Many people in Pennsylvania and many of his old Federalist friends were strong supporters of the bank. Yet Jackson, the leader of Buchanan's party, was the bank's greatest enemy. Being in Russia, Buchanan did not have to choose one side or the other.

By the time Buchanan arrived as the new senator from Pennsylvania, politicians were already talking about the 1836 presidential election. Jackson would be retiring, but he urged the party to nominate his vice president, Martin Van Buren. Jackson and Van Buren had reorganized the party and renamed it the Democratic party. The main opposition came from a new political party, the Whigs, who had organized to fight Andrew Jackson and the Democrats.

Soon after Van Buren took office in 1837, the country was struck by a severe "panic," or recession. Farmers lost their land, small merchants went bankrupt, and banks across the country failed. Prices rose rapidly, and many people in cities went hungry. There was a great clamor for Van Buren and Congress to do something to help the suffering and end the panic. In the congressional elections of 1838, the Whigs made huge gains.

In 1840, Van Buren was nominated for a second term as president. The Whigs nominated William Henry Harrison, a war hero nicknamed "Old Tippecanoe." Van Buren was very unpopular and many voters were eager for a change. The Whigs carried the election, electing Harrison president and gaining majorities in Congress. That left the Democrats, including Buchanan, in the minority.

Buchanan worked with other Democrats in the Senate to oppose Whig plans to increase the power of the federal government. At the same time, he worked against southern Democrats like John C. Calhoun, who wanted to weaken the federal government and give more power to the states. He continued to seek a middle way between the two extreme points of view. He also served as chairman of the Senate Committee on Foreign Relations, where he was able to keep up his knowledge of world affairs.

Home Life

During his years in the Senate, Buchanan's family situation grew very complicated. He spent part of each year in Lancaster when the Senate was not in session. By this time, his sisters and surviving brother had families, all of whom saw him as the "rich uncle" who could help them out during difficult times. Buchanan did his best to take care of them. Several of his sisters died, and he stepped in to provide financial and other support for his young nieces and nephews.

James Buchanan about 1840.

By 1841, his eight-year-old nephew, James Buchanan Henry, and his eleven-year-old niece, Harriet Lane, moved into the old Coleman mansion in Lancaster. Buchanan was there part of each year, and Miss Hetty cared for them when Buchanan was in Washington. Buchanan bought new furniture for several rooms in the house and gave Miss Hetty extra money for higher household expenses.

Uncle Buchanan was a kind man to his nieces and nephews. He made sure that they were well cared for and sent them to good schools. He also helped out his brother and sisters. They were grateful for his help, but they sometimes resented his success and his wealth. For the rest of his life Buchanan took on the responsibility of caring for his family, just as his father had predicted many years before.

Secretary of State

As the 1844 election approached, Buchanan set out to win the presidential nomination of the Democratic party. He worked quietly behind the scenes, asking for support from his many friends and associates in Washington. Unfortunately for Buchanan, the most powerful man in the party was still Martin Van Buren, who had helped to send Buchanan to Russia twelve years earlier.

The way of nominating candidates for president had changed. Now the Democrats gathered at a national convention to choose candidates for president and vice president. When they met in the summer of 1844, Van Buren was the favorite. When he couldn't gain the required two-thirds of the vote, Lewis Cass of Michigan went ahead. But Cass couldn't gain two-thirds of the votes either. On the 14th *ballot* (or vote), former Tennessee congressman James K. Polk was nominated as a compromise candidate. Buchanan had scarcely been mentioned. Worse yet, the convention chose Buchanan's Pennsylvania rival George Dallas as the vice presidential candidate.

Despite his disappointment, Buchanan worked hard to carry Pennsylvania for Polk and Dallas in the November election. They were elected. Soon afterward, Polk appointed James Buchanan *secretary of state*, the official who manages the country's foreign relations and diplomacy. After ten years in the Senate, Buchanan was pleased and flattered to accept the new position. He rented an elegant Washington house that would allow him to entertain visiting diplomats from around the world. With his new duties, he would spend much less time in Lancaster.

Polk had won the election partly because he was a strong supporter of plans to *annex* Texas, making it part of the United States. Texas, formerly a part

The "Grand Democratic Banner" for the 1844 presidential election, showing candidates James K. Polk and George Dallas.

Circular.

Department of State
Washington, March 10, 1845

I have the honor to inform you that the President, by and with the advice and consent of the Senate, has appointed me Secretary of State of the United States, and that I have this day entered upon the duties of that office.

I am, Sir,
Your obedient servant,

James Buchanan

This "circular," signed by Buchanan, announces that he has taken up his duties as secretary of state.

of Mexico, was now an independent republic that wanted to join the Union. Congress made Texas a U.S. territory even before Polk took office in March 1845. Mexico still claimed the region, however, and was threatening to declare war. As secretary of state, Buchanan began searching for a way to end the dispute with Mexico peacefully.

At the same time, President Polk began tough negotiations with Great Britain over the region called Oregon. For nearly 30 years, Britain and the United States had jointly managed the great northwestern territory between the Pacific Ocean and the Rocky Mountains. Now that many U.S. citizens were settling in the region, Polk wanted to gain undisputed control of it. As secretary of state, Buchanan was given responsibility for those negotiations.

Buchanan proposed that the two countries compromise, with the United States taking the southern part and the British the north. Then President Polk announced that the United States wanted *all* of the region, from the California border up to the border with the Russian territory of Alaska. Americans in favor of expansion cheered the president's demands. Britain was outraged and began to fit out warships to send to the Pacific.

Buchanan prepared an agreement in which the United States claimed the whole region. Then President Polk changed his mind again, and agreed to the

This cartoon makes fun of James Polk's demand for all of the Oregon country. John Bull, representing Great Britain, says, "What, you young Yankee-noodle, strike your own father?"

compromise Buchanan had proposed earlier. The British, who were not eager to go to war over the distant wilderness, quickly agreed. Buchanan was relieved at avoiding war, but he was unhappy that the president was making all the decisions. In the final treaty, the United States gained undisputed control of the land in present-day Washington, Oregon, and Idaho, and parts of Montana and Wyoming. Britain gained undisputed claim to present-day British Columbia.

Texas

In December 1845, Congress approved making Texas a state, and President Polk signed the bill into law. Knowing that Mexico was threatening war, he sent troops to the Texas border with Mexico. The boundary between the two nations was disputed, and when Americans built a fort on land that Mexico claimed, Mexican troops fired on the Americans. In May 1846, Congress declared war at the request of President Polk.

For the next two years, American armies led by generals Zachary Taylor and Winfield Scott battled Mexican forces. Americans invaded northern Mexico near the Texas border, sent an expedition to the Mexican territory of New Mexico, and set up a pro-American government in Mexico's territory of Upper California. Then they invaded central Mexico and marched toward the country's capital,

Mexico City. U.S. troops were far better equipped than the Mexicans and won every battle they fought. Mexico City finally surrendered in September 1847. In the peace negotiations, the United States demanded and received nearly 500,000 square miles (1.3 million km^2), including the present-day states of California, Arizona, Nevada, Utah, and New Mexico, and parts of five other states.

Although Buchanan was well equipped to serve as secretary of state, he was unhappy in the job. President Polk made important diplomatic decisions without consulting him, then left Buchanan to work out the details. Buchanan also discovered that as a cabinet member he had very little political power of his own. Even in Pennsylvania, appointments to federal government positions were decided by his rival, Vice President Dallas.

A New Campaign

As the election of 1848 approached, Buchanan was once again seeking the presidential nomination. Polk had pledged not to run for a second term, so the nomination was open. Once again, however, Buchanan was disappointed. The Democrats nominated Lewis Cass of Michigan. The Whigs nominated Zachary Taylor, a hero of the U.S.-Mexican War. In addition, former president Martin Van Buren ran on the Free-Soil ticket, representing northern voters who wanted to end the spread of slavery. In the three-way election, Whig Zachary Taylor was elected.

Buchanan was out of work. He had resigned from the Senate to serve as secretary of state. With a new Whig president, he could not expect an appointment to the cabinet. Buchanan retired to his home in Lancaster.

Chapter 4

Returning Home

Buchanan was no longer a dashing young lawyer. He was a dignified white-haired gentleman. Still, there was a twinkle in Buchanan's eyes and a spring to his step. He still had the lifelong habit of cocking his head to one side when speaking to someone. Even though he had retired from the Senate and no longer served on the president's cabinet, he still lived and breathed politics. The ambition to become president still burned inside him.

For now, however, his immediate attention was drawn to his family. By this time, he had 22 nieces and nephews and 13 grandnieces and grandnephews. Seven of the children were orphans under his guardianship, and others had only one surviving parent.

His first order of business upon returning to Lancaster was to find a bigger house. In the summer of 1848, Buchanan bought a beautiful estate called Wheatland. The large red brick mansion was

Wheatland, the estate Buchanan bought near Lancaster, Pennsylvania, in 1848. Today it is a museum that preserves and displays Buchanan memorabilia.

surrounded by rolling lands and fields. The property included a barn and several

outbuildings. By the spring of 1849, the house was furnished and ready. Buchanan

and his housekeeper, Miss Hetty, moved in and settled into a comfortable, relaxed

routine. He spent hours writing letters at his enormous desk in the library. In the

afternoons he entertained visitors or walked around the grounds. In the evenings he

might share a glass of wine with friends or write long into the night. Many times

Miss Hetty found him slumped over his desk asleep.

Wheatland had been built as a summer home. That winter, Buchanan realized that it was difficult to keep warm, so he installed a new furnace. He later built a new kitchen and made other renovations. Soon Wheatland was as comfortable and homelike as anyone could wish. Buchanan considered it his home for the rest of his life, and he proudly accepted the nickname that his political friends gave him: "the Sage of Wheatland." He once said that if he could be reincarnated after death, he would like to come back as a frog so that he could live near the spring at Wheatland. Today there is a small statue of a frog sitting where the spring once flowed.

Vivacious Harriet and Stubborn Buck ———

Buchanan was the father figure and guardian to two family orphans, Harriet Lane and James Buchanan Henry, nicknamed "Buck." Harriet was the youngest daughter of Buchanan's sister Jane. Throughout her childhood and adolescence, Buchanan sent her to a succession of boarding schools. She spent her summers with the families of Buchanan's friends, although he kept a close eye on her from Washington.

As a girl, Harriet was a spirited tomboy. Buchanan loved Harriet dearly, but he was shocked at her unladylike behavior, often scolding her for her boisterous ways. She continued to get into trouble at school, once for secretly writing letters to a boy. Finally Buchanan enrolled her in the strict Visitation Convent School in Washington, D.C. When Buchanan moved into Wheatland, Harriet was 19 years old. She had finished school, but was traveling with friends. When she returned, she took on the role of lady of the house and hostess to the visitors and well-wishers.

Buck Buchanan had been in his uncle's care since he was seven. He was the son of Buchanan's sister Harriet. He had lived with Miss Hetty in Lancaster while Buchanan was in Washington. Buck was at boarding school when Buchanan bought Wheatland, but he returned to spend his summers on the estate. Buck was a stubborn boy, and Buchanan could never persuade him to behave or even to eat his vegetables. In 1851, Buck enrolled in the College of New Jersey (now Princeton University). When he graduated, he went to study law with Buchanan's friend John Cadwalader in Philadelphia.

Return to Politics

In 1851, Buchanan began another quiet campaign for the 1852 Democratic presidential nomination. He wrote many letters, urging his supporters to speak in his behalf. The major issue was slavery.

In 1850, Congress had passed a wide-reaching compromise intended to settle the vexing arguments between North and South. For those who opposed the spread of slavery, the Compromise of 1850 admitted California to the Union as a free state. For 30 years, states had been admitted in pairs—one state that permitted slavery and one free state. This kept an exact balance between slave and free states and between proslavery and antislavery senators in the U.S. Senate. California's admission tipped the balance of free and slave states for the first time. For supporters of slavery, the compromise included a tough new Fugitive Slave Act. It committed the federal government to help return slaves who had run away to the North to their owners in the South.

Far from ending arguments over slavery, the Compromise of 1850 only made them worse. Southerners were angry that there were now more free states than slave states. Northerners were infuriated by the Fugitive Slave Act, which made it a crime for a northerner to give any help to a runaway slave.

As the Democratic nominating convention approached, the two leading contenders for the presidential nomination were Senator Stephen Douglas, who had helped pass the compromise, and James Buchanan. Convention delegates were so divided that neither candidate could gain the required number of votes. After many ballots, a delegate from New Hampshire nominated the state's former senator, Franklin Pierce. Pierce had been out of politics for ten years and had few enemies. The weary delegates agreed to support this "dark horse" candidate and nominated him to run for president. Once again, James Buchanan failed to gain his party's nomination.

Henry Clay outlines the Compromise of 1850 to the Senate. The compromise measures were approved in September 1850 and signed by President Millard Fillmore.

Franklin Pierce won election in November 1852. When he took office the following year, he appointed Buchanan minister to Great Britain. Once again, Buchanan was being asked to travel far from the Washington political scene. He was reluctant to accept the position. Still, he was deeply interested in foreign affairs and had no better choice, so he finally agreed.

He wound up his affairs at Wheatland, then set sail for England. Harriet joined him a few months later. She soon caused a sensation in the British capital. Her liveliness, intelligence, and poise quickly won over the proper English. Queen Victoria liked Harriet so much that she offered the young American every courtesy, even encouraging her to dance with her beloved husband, Prince Albert. Buchanan's work as minister was less successful. Relations between the United States and Great Britain were chilly. Buchanan made many personal friends, but he was not able to overcome the two countries' disagreements.

In 1854, he became embroiled in a more dangerous matter. President Pierce had hoped to buy the island of Cuba from Spain. When his minister to Spain failed to get Spain to agree, Pierce arranged a meeting between Buchanan and the U.S. ministers to Spain and France to review the situation. They sent a memorandum to the president recommending that the United States force Spain to agree to the sale. If Spain refused to sell Cuba, the memorandum said, the United States might find it necessary to take over the island by force.

Franklin Pierce, the Democratic "dark horse" candidate who was elected president in 1852.

★ GENTLEMAN FARMER ★

The document became known as the Ostend Manifesto (for the city in present-day Belgium where the ministers met). When parts of it were published in U.S. newspapers, northerners protested bitterly. They believed that President Pierce and his southern supporters wanted to make Cuba a new slave state in the United States. The outcry was so great that Pierce denied responsibility for the document and said that it did not represent the government's policy. Northerners blamed Buchanan and the other ministers for the offensive document. More than a hundred years later, historians discovered that President Pierce himself had ordered his ministers to include the threat of war in the manifesto.

Unsuccessful in Great Britain and damaged by the Ostend Manifesto, Buchanan offered the president his resignation in 1855. In early 1856, he returned once more to Wheatland. The presidential election of 1856 was approaching. Buchanan was almost 65 years old. He knew that this would be his last chance to win the presidency.

Violence at Home

While Buchanan was in England, the country had become even more bitterly divided on the question of slavery. In 1854, Senator Stephen Douglas had proposed another compromise to calm the growing strife. With the support of President Pierce, he gained passage of the Kansas-Nebraska Act. The act established boundaries for the new territories of Kansas and Nebraska west of the Missouri River. It provided that the residents of these territories would decide for themselves whether to permit slavery by voting on proposed state constitutions.

The bill had strong support among Democrats, especially in the South. Members of the new Republican party and many northern Democrats were horrified. The Missouri Compromise, passed 34 years earlier, had specifically provided that the region including Kansas and Nebraska would be free of slavery. Now the Kansas-Nebraska Act threatened to allow slavery to spread to these territories.

Antislavery groups in the North sent new settlers to Kansas to vote for an antislavery constitution. Southerners sent settlers to vote in favor of slavery and encouraged residents of neighboring Missouri, a slave state, to cross into Kansas to vote. When a vote on the constitution was taken, many voters were threatened or refused entrance to the polling places. Hundreds of nonresidents appeared and cast their votes without trouble. Soon two governments were operating in the territory, one proslavery and the other antislavery. In 1856, a proslavery "posse" terrorized the antislavery town of Lawrence, destroying a

Proslavery and antislavery forces in Kansas fought for control of the state during the 1850s.

The attack by Congressman Preston Brooks of South Carolina on Massachusetts Senator Charles Sumner in May 1856.

hotel and wrecking the printing presses of antislavery newspapers. Days later, a raiding party led by John Brown, a radical antislavery leader, killed five proslavery farmers.

Violence even spread to Washington. After Senator Charles Sumner of Massachusetts had made a bitter speech against southern senators, Congressman Preston Brooks, whose uncle was one of the senators Sumner insulted, stormed onto the Senate floor and beat Sumner with a cane until he was unconscious. Sumner was so badly injured that he did not return to his duties for many months.

Once again, Buchanan was lucky to escape this stormy time in Washington. Because he was in Great Britain, he had not become embroiled in the ugly Kansas-Nebraska debate, and he still had friends on both sides. As a distinguished diplomat and former senator, he was seen as an elder statesman. His absence from Washington now gave him his best chance at the presidency.

At the Democratic convention, Buchanan finally won his party's nomination for president with the enthusiastic support of southern leaders. The Democratic party remained home to proslavery southerners and to northerners who were still hoping for a compromise that would save the Union.

In the election, Buchanan faced opponents from new political parties. The old Whig party had fallen apart in 1854, hopelessly divided by the Kansas-

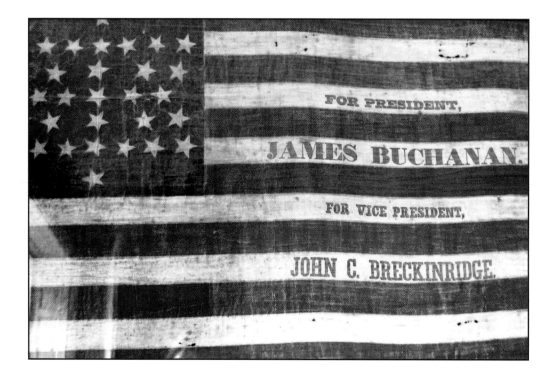

A flag for Buchanan and Breckinridge used in the 1856 presidential campaign.

Nebraska Act. In its place, the new Republican party had arisen. Its members were almost all in the North, and its platform opposed the spread of slavery to any new territories. The party's first presidential candidate was John C. Frémont. A third party, the American party, was also running its first candidate. Nicknamed the "Know-Nothings," American party members campaigned against immigrants and Roman Catholics. They nominated former Whig president Millard Fillmore.

In the style of the day, Buchanan did not campaign actively. He stayed at Wheatland throughout the summer, writing hundreds of letters and meeting with dozens of politicians, supporters, and newspaper writers. In November, Buchanan led all candidates in the popular vote and won the election. Still, the voting results showed how divided the country was. Buchanan received less than 46 percent of the vote. Together, his two opponents received 54 percent.

Chapter 5

A Presidency Crippled by Slavery

First Steps ———————————————

In his inaugural address on March 4, 1857, James Buchanan continued the theme he had set forth in the campaign: "Save the Union." He spoke with special feeling against the *abolitionists*, a group that saw slavery as a grave moral issue and insisted that it be ended immediately. In his mind, slavery was a legal and constitutional issue. The U.S. Constitution recognized the right of men to own slaves. In addition, the Constitution gave each state the power over its own laws and customs. Northern abolitionists had no right to interfere with slavery in the South. Buchanan also knew that southern states would *secede* (leave the Union) if antislavery forces tried to meddle in their affairs. He urged the North to accept the compromises of the past in order to save the Union. He knew that both sides were angry, but he believed there was still room for compromise.

After the solemn inauguration ceremony, there was time for celebration. Thousands of people jammed into a specially constructed building that evening for the inaugural ball. Guests danced under a ceiling festooned with gold stars and ate a feast of meats, jellies, ice cream, and a cake four feet (1.2 meters) high. Buchanan's niece Harriet Lane appeared in a beautiful white gown, and her

James Buchanan and his niece Harriet Lane (at left) at the inaugural ball in March 1857.

dazzling smile and gracious manners won many admirers. She would serve as the official White House hostess during her uncle's term of office.

Dred Scott ───────────────────────

Two days after Buchanan took office, the U.S. Supreme Court announced one of the most important and explosive decisions in its history. Dred Scott was an African American who had been born into slavery in Missouri. When he was a young man, he went with his master to live in the free state of Illinois and later in the free territories of Minnesota and Wisconsin. After they returned to Missouri, Scott sued the government for his freedom, claiming that the time he lived in regions that outlawed slavery had made him free.

The Supreme Court announced that it would not consider Scott's case. As a black man and a slave, the court said, Scott was not a citizen of the United States and had no right to bring a lawsuit. The time spent in free states and territories had no bearing on his condition. He remained a slave with "no rights that a white man is bound to respect."

The court further expressed its belief that the Missouri Compromise of 1820, which outlawed slavery in much of the West (including the Kansas and Nebraska territories) was unconstitutional. In fact, it believed that the federal government had no right to prohibit or restrict slavery in new territories.

Slave Dred Scott (left) sued in federal court for his freedom. Chief Justice Roger Taney (right) ruled that as a slave, Scott had no rights and must remain a slave.

President Buchanan welcomed the decision. He believed that it settled the legal standing of slavery, and he urged the people of the United States to respect and obey it. He was surprised by the firestorm of anger and defiance the decision caused in the northern states. Like the earlier Compromise of 1850 and the Kansas-Nebraska Act, the Dred Scott decision increased anger and dissension in the country.

Kansas

The president was also faced with a more practical problem in Kansas. In a further effort to establish a legitimate government and move toward statehood, another vote was held on a constitution proposed by the proslavery government at Lecompton. Antislavery forces in the state refused to participate in the vote, and the proslavery constitution was approved. Should the federal government accept the constitution and admit Kansas as a slave state?

Once again, Buchanan decided the issue on legal grounds. He reasoned that the vote had been legal and that its result should be honored. Privately, he believed that antislavery forces in Kansas could change their constitution after it became a state. He recommended to Congress that Kansas be admitted to the Union under the proslavery constitution it submitted. Democrats had a majority in both houses of Congress, and he was hopeful they would agree.

Buchanan ran into opposition from his own party. Senator Douglas, who had written the Kansas-Nebraska Act, announced that the vote for the Lecompton constitution had been a fraud. He was against admitting Kansas to the Union until a fair vote could be arranged. In the Senate, Democrats approved the admission of Kansas even against Douglas's advice. In the House of Representatives, however, northern congressmen, including many Democrats, refused to pass the bill for Kansas statehood. They proposed a complicated compromise instead.

The States During the Presidency of James Buchanan

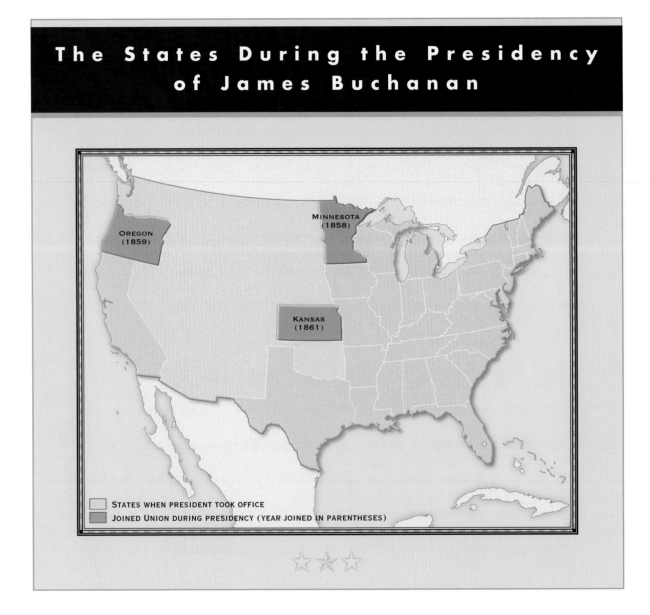

OREGON
(1859)

MINNESOTA
(1858)

KANSAS
(1861)

STATES WHEN PRESIDENT TOOK OFFICE
JOINED UNION DURING PRESIDENCY (YEAR JOINED IN PARENTHESES)

Buchanan had failed to carry his proposal, and he was criticized in the North and South alike. People on both sides were angry about Kansas, and now they could put some of the blame on the president.

The Panic of 1857

As if the Dred Scott decision and the Kansas controversy weren't enough, Buchanan also faced tough economic times. In 1857, the stock market crashed, banks closed, businesses failed, and farmers lost their farms. In northern cities, workers took to the streets, chanting, "Bread or blood!"

People clamored for the president to take some action to ease the depression and give aid to those who were suffering from it. Like earlier presidents, Buchanan did not have the power to address the causes of the depression. He made matters worse, however, by seeming to be uncaring about the human suffering the bad times were causing. He scolded those who lost their money on investments in stocks. If they had invested more wisely, they would not have lost, he said. His attitude seemed cold and unfeeling and further reduced his popularity.

In the midterm elections for Congress in 1858, voters in the North made their disapproval of Buchanan clear. Republicans, who opposed many of his policies, gained a majority in Congress. They would make his last two years in office even more difficult.

Calm Within White House Walls

At the end of his stressful days, Buchanan gladly looked for the calm comforts of the White House. Buchanan and Harriet hosted small weekly dinner parties for his cabinet members, colleagues, and their families. They threw elaborate parties. Even in these dark times, members of Washington society eagerly awaited invitations to a White House event.

Harriet proved to be a gracious and popular first lady. She successfully coordinated a reception for the first Japanese delegation ever to visit the United States. When the Prince of Wales visited, Harriet planned a boat ride on the Potomac, an afternoon game of ninepins, and a dinner party. Although the president banned dancing and card playing in the White House, Harriet still managed to entertain with style.

A photograph of Harriet Lane during her time as official White House hostess.

☆ ★ ☆

Foreign Affairs ———————————————————————

As a former diplomat and secretary of state, Buchanan had hoped to pursue an active foreign policy as president. Because of the pressing problems at home, however, he was forced to put foreign policy near the bottom of his agenda. Many of his more ambitious plans were frustrated by growing opposition in Congress. He proposed another effort to buy Cuba from Spain, but antislavery forces in the North refused to consider the plan. He also proposed buying Alaska from Russia, but all attention was focused on the growing problems at home.

Buchanan did manage to improve relations with Great Britain, coming to agreement about the two countries' interests and actions in Central America. He also supervised the creation of new trade agreements with China and Japan, opening new trade opportunities for American traders and merchants.

Harper's Ferry ———————————————————————

As Buchanan struggled through the third year of his presidency, he had lost much of his support. His hope of bringing North and South together was fading. Voters had elected a Republican Congress hostile to his views. Northern Democrats, led by his rival Stephen Douglas, had refused to support many of his policies. His lifelong habit of avoiding conflict and his deep belief in settling matters by compromise were hurting him.

Buchanan was personally caring and thoughtful, and privately he expressed compassion for slaves as individuals. However, his success in politics had always come from following the Constitution, which seemed to allow slavery. He believed the first duty of a president was to "see that the laws are faithfully executed." It was the job of Congress to change the laws. In addition, Buchanan was so eager to keep the country together that he seemed not to grasp the deep anxiety of the people over the slavery issue.

Then in 1859, another crisis arose. On the morning of October 16, abolitionist John Brown, with an "army" of 18 men (13 whites and 5 African Americans), attacked a federal *arsenal*, a storage place for weapons and ammunition, in Harper's Ferry, Virginia (now West Virginia). The mountain town was only 30 miles (48 km) from the White House. Brown's little band succeeded in capturing the arsenal, but were disappointed when local slaves did not join their call to begin a slave uprising. Local militia soon attacked the arsenal, killing some of Brown's "soldiers." Brown escaped, but the next day, he and his remaining men were cornered by federal troops. Brown, badly wounded, was imprisoned. Later in October, he was tried, convicted of treason and murder, and sentenced to death. On December 2, he was hanged.

The raid on Harper's Ferry seemed to divide the country once and for all. Southerners were outraged when they learned that Brown had received financial

The execution of John Brown, who was convicted of treason and murder, in December 1859.

help and approval from the "Secret Six," a group of wealthy northerners in the abolitionist movement. How could sane, rational people plot rebellion and cold-blooded murder? Southerners saw the raid as proof that antislavery forces were intent on destroying slavery and the South.

At the same time, the raid strengthened the Republican party in the North because it focused attention on the morality of slavery. What were President

Who Was John Brown?

It is difficult to imagine how deeply the actions of John Brown moved the people of the United States in 1859.

Brown grew up in a deeply religious family that was strongly opposed to slavery. His father was an early abolitionist who preached that slavery was a moral wrong that must be ended. Brown married twice and raised a large family. They moved often, and Brown held many different jobs, including farmer, tanner, and wool merchant. His sons moved to Kansas during the slavery disputes there, and John Brown joined them. In 1856, he led a party that massacred proslavery farmers.

Even though he was wanted for murder in Kansas, Brown continued to travel freely through the North, and he met with some of America's most respected writers and thinkers, discussing his militant opposition to slavery and his plan for a "war" against it.

In October 1859, he led the raid on the Harper's Ferry arsenal and was soon captured. Reports of his trial were published in newspapers around the country. Southerners believed he was an evil man who had committed treason against his country. His defense tried to claim that he was insane. In the North, many were moved by his dignified behavior at the trial, and they mourned his death by hanging. Not long afterward, at antislavery rallies people were singing new words to the tune we know as "The Battle Hymn of the Republic":

John Brown's body lies a mould'ring in the grave,

But his soul is marching on.

Glory, glory hallelujah,

His soul is marching on.

★ ★ ☆

A portrait of John Brown, who was hated by many in the South and considered a martyred hero by abolitionists in the North.

A photograph of James Buchanan during his presidency.

Buchanan's legal arguments worth if slavery was morally hateful and wrong? Many antislavery activists admired John Brown's courage in risking everything to destroy slavery and to free slaves.

The Election of 1860 ————————————

As 1860 dawned, political parties began preparing for the presidential election in November. By this time it was clear that slavery was the only issue that mattered.

The Republicans met in Chicago. They nominated Illinois lawyer Abraham Lincoln, who was the most eloquent critic of Democratic policies on slavery. He and his party stood firm in the belief that slavery should not be allowed in the new territories. The Republicans also appealed to northern merchants and businessmen by favoring more federal funds for roads, bridges, and other improvements.

James Buchanan had pledged to serve one term. In 1860, no Democrats asked him to change his mind. The party convention met in Charleston, South Carolina. The two strongest prospects for president were Buchanan's old opponent Stephen Douglas and Vice President John Breckinridge from Kentucky. The party was so divided over slavery and other sectional disputes that it could not agree on a platform or a candidate. The convention nominated Douglas, but southern delegates walked out of the convention and nominated Breckinridge. Buchanan refused to support Douglas as the party's nominee, helping to split the party.

In November, Lincoln and the Republicans carried the northern states and gained a majority of the electoral vote to win election. Douglas ran strongly in the North, where many voters were still afraid of the antislavery Republicans.

Breckinridge split the southern vote with a third-party candidate. Lincoln was elected president, but he received less than 40 percent of the popular vote. The two Democrats together won nearly 48 percent.

Secession

As soon as the election results were known, southern political leaders condemned the incoming president and his party. Southern states had already discussed seceding from the United States to be free of the hated antislavery agitation in the North. A Buchanan supporter wrote to him, "I see no possibility of preserving the Union."

In December 1860, South Carolina became the first southern state to secede. By early February, six other states had followed—Mississippi, Florida, Alabama, Georgia, Louisiana, and Texas.

As the Union fell apart, so did Buchanan's administration. Four of his cabinet members, all slave-owners from the South, resigned and went home. The country waited fearfully to see what would happen next. Soon after South Carolina seceded, its state militia began to seize all federal property in the state, including arsenals and military bases. Only at Fort Sumter, an island in the Charleston harbor, were federal troops still at their posts.

Would President Buchanan send reinforcements to the federal fort? He conferred with Congress, which refused to vote funds for an expedition. Rather than dispute its decision, he dropped the idea. As the garrison ran short of food, its commander, Major Robert Anderson, requested supplies. Buchanan ordered a supply ship to Fort Sumter. As it approached the fort, however, South Carolina forces fired on it, and it was forced to withdraw. The uneasy standoff between Union troops inside Fort Sumter and South Carolina forces on the mainland became a symbol of the tensions in the country.

As southern states seceded, their congressmen and senators resigned and went home to their states. Among them

THE BEWILDERED OLD WOMAN.

During Buchanan's last year as president, magazines in the North ridiculed him. This cruel political cartoon shows Buchanan as a confused old woman. The caption says, "Sakes alive! I know no North, no South, no East, no West—no nothing!"

were many of Buchanan's supporters. The remaining members of Congress, especially the Republican majority, saw no reason to cooperate with the president. Increasingly isolated and powerless, he continued to seek ways to recover the situation. He proposed to President-Elect Lincoln that they jointly call a constitutional convention to discuss the deep divisions between the states. Lincoln politely refused.

There was one piece of good news during Buchanan's last days in the White House. Kansas had withdrawn the proslavery Lecompton constitution. Its leaders had prepared a constitution that prohibited slavery, and in a fair vote, it was approved by a large majority of voters. This allowed them to apply officially for statehood as a free state. Congress (now without many of its southern members) approved its application, and Buchanan signed the act on January 29, 1861, a few weeks before he left office.

Buchanan worked until his last day in office to keep other southern states from seceding and to avoid any incident that might set off a war. In these two small tasks he succeeded, but he was eager to go home. On March 4, 1861, he rode in a carriage with Abraham Lincoln to Lincoln's inauguration. Buchanan said to Lincoln, "My dear sir, if you are as happy in entering the White House as I shall feel on returning to Wheatland, you are a happy man indeed."

Chapter 6

Happy Homecoming —————————

When Buchanan arrived home in Lancaster in 1861, he was warmly greeted by a large crowd of well-wishers, pealing church bells, and a parade. He made a brief speech that put into words his happiness at returning home, saying, "I have no language to express the feelings which swell in my heart [but] cordially thank you for this demonstration of your personal kindness to an old man, who comes back to you."

Buchanan basked in the joy of living once again at Wheatland. For the first month after his arrival home, he took long walks, read, and received visitors and well-wishers. Musical groups played evening concerts. It was the beginning of a deserved retirement for a man who had spent most of his life in public service. Unfortunately, even his retirement was destined to be stormy.

First Shots Begin the War —————————————

On April 12, 1861, Confederate guns opened fire on Fort Sumter, beginning the Civil War. All the hostility and anger between North and South would now find its voice in battle. Hundreds of thousands of Americans would die, and much of the South would be reduced to rubble. Searching for someone to blame, Republicans and others pointed to Buchanan. Some of his former cabinet members, now in Lincoln's cabinet, took part in the accusations.

Even in Lancaster, people warned that Buchanan should not show his face in town. He began receiving violent, hate-filled letters. Miss Hetty found notes threatening to burn down Wheatland stuck to the back door. Buchanan was so shocked by the sudden attacks that he suffered an attack of bilious fever and was bedridden for a time.

Seeking to defend himself, Buchanan began to write a book explaining his actions as president. Called *Mr. Buchanan's Administration on the Eve of the Rebellion*, it was published in 1866, soon after the war ended. By that time, a war-weary public was not very interested in Buchanan's explanations.

Despite the criticism and accusations, Buchanan's friends and leading Democrats paid visits to him at Wheatland during his retirement. After the war ended, he received visits from old friends from the southern states. They brought much sad news of sons and brothers killed in the war, and the destruction of

On April 12, 1861, Confederate cannon in Charleston, South Carolina, fired on Fort Sumter in the Charleston harbor, where federal troops were stationed. These were the first shots of the Civil War.

homes and livelihoods. Buchanan ached for the misery the war had caused for both sides.

A bright spot in Buchanan's retirement was his reunion with his family. He entertained his many nieces and nephews and their children and grandchildren. Harriet was traveling much of the time, but returned to Wheatland for visits. Buchanan's niece Annie Buchanan also spent time with her uncle. Buck Buchanan was married and living in New York.

In 1866, Harriet was married to Henry E. Johnston of Baltimore in a ceremony at Wheatland. Buchanan liked Johnston, saying that he was a gentleman with a good education, good manners, and an excellent character.

Two years after Harriet's marriage, in May of 1868, Buchanan became ill. As his condition worsened, he realized that the end was near. Friends and family members came to pay their last visits, and Buchanan gave them detailed instructions as to how to manage his affairs. He chose a burial site and a plain white marble tombstone.

Tragedy in Harriet's Life

At Wheatland today there hangs a painting of two little boys sitting on a rocky ledge overlooking the sea. The boys are Harriet's children, James and Henry. James was born in 1866, and named after his grand-uncle. Henry was born four years later.

Sadly, young James died of a fever in 1881 before his 15th birthday. Henry died a year later, in 1882, when he was twelve. The painting was probably made after the boys had died, as a reminder of their lives. Many Victorian families commissioned these portraits as an attempt to soften the grief of death. The water in the painting is a symbol that the boys have died and made the voyage to another shore.

☆ ★ ☆

Even through his final illness, Buchanan continued to insist that history would prove that he was a good president and a good politician. The night before his death, he told a friend that he believed he had done everything in his power to discharge his public duties well. He had no regrets for any public act.

On Monday morning, June 1, 1868, Buchanan died. He was 77 years old. He had requested a simple funeral, but thousands traveled to Wheatland to walk past his casket and pay their last respects. Many more attended his funeral on Thursday, including political leaders from across the nation. At the funeral, his friend, Dr. John Nevin, reminded listeners of Buchanan's strengths. "He has served his country well," Dr. Nevin said. "He has left behind him a fair example of justice, benevolence, integrity and truth, a bright record indeed, of honorable and virtuous character in all respects."

James Buchanan was buried in a cemetery near Lancaster. Later a plain white marble memorial was placed over the grave.

Buchanan's Legacy

The approaching war over slavery and states' rights overshadowed Buchanan's presidency from beginning to end. He was an intelligent man and a skilled lawyer. Yet he believed so strongly in the law that he could not find a way to calm

HERE REST THE REMAINS OF
JAMES BUCHANAN
FIFTEENTH PRESIDENT OF THE UNITED STATES.
BORN IN FRANKLIN COUNTY, PA. APRIL 23, 1791.
DIED AT WHEATLAND, JUNE 1, 1868.

Buchanan's tombstone, which identifies him simply as the 15th President of the United States and gives the places and dates of his birth and death.

the fierce anger and hatreds of the slavery debate. Buchanan hoped that one day historians would recognize that he was a good president, but that hope has not been realized. In a recent survey of historians, Buchanan was ranked 41st of the first 42 presidents in effectiveness.

Buchanan was not responsible for the Civil War, as some of his enemies claimed. He did not cause the deepening anger and suspicion between North and South. Yet it is clear that Buchanan was not strong enough or wise enough to avoid the approaching storm. Perhaps in a quieter time his particular talents would have made him more effective. In the dark times of the 1850s, however, he did not succeed.

Fast Facts James Buchanan

Birth:	April 23, 1791
Birthplace:	Cove Gap, Pennsylvania
Parents:	James and Elizabeth Speer Buchanan
Brothers & Sisters:	Mary (1789–1791)
	Jane (1793–1839)
	Maria (1795–1849)
	Sarah (1798–1825)
	Elizabeth (1800–1801)
	Harriet (1802–1840)
	John (1804–1804)
	William Speer (1805–1826)
	George Washington (1808–1832)
	Edward (1811–1895)
Education:	Dickinson College, Carlisle, Pennsylvania; graduated 1809
Occupation:	Lawyer
Marriage:	None (his niece Harriet Lane served as first lady in the White House)
Political Parties:	Federalist, Democratic-Republican, Democratic
Public Offices:	1815–1816 Pennsylvania General Assembly
	1821–1831 U.S. House of Representatives
	1832–1833 U.S. Minister to Russia
	1834–1845 U.S. Senate
	1845–1849 Secretary of State (under President James K. Polk)
	1853–1856 U.S. Minister to Great Britain
	1857–1861 15th President of the United States
His Vice President:	John Breckinridge
Major Actions as President:	1857 Endorsed the Dred Scott decision by the Supreme Court, recognizing the legal basis of slavery
	1858 Recommended that Congress approve the proslavery Lecompton constitution and admit Kansas as a slave state
	1861 Signed bill admitting Kansas as a free (nonslave) state
Firsts:	First president who never married
	First president born and raised in Pennsylvania
Death:	June 1, 1868
Age at Death:	77 years
Burial Place:	Woodward Hill Cemetery, Lancaster, Pennsylvania

Fast Facts Harriet Lane

Birth:	May 9, 1830
Birthplace:	Mercersburg, Pennsylvania
Parents:	Elliot Tole and Jane Buchanan Lane (Jane Buchanan was President Buchanan's younger sister)
Education:	Boarding schools, including the Visitation Convent School, Washington, D.C.
Served as First Lady:	1857–1861, during the presidency of her uncle, James Buchanan
Marriage:	To Henry Elliot Johnston II, January 11, 1866
Children:	James Buchanan Johnston (1866–1881)
	Henry Elliot Johnston (1870–1882)
Firsts:	Three U.S. Navy cutters have been named for her
	Established the Harriet Lane Home for Invalid Children, which continues today as the children's wing of Johns Hopkins Hospital in Baltimore, Maryland
Death:	July 3, 1903
Age at Death:	73 years
Burial Place:	Greenmont Cemetery, Baltimore, Maryland

Timeline

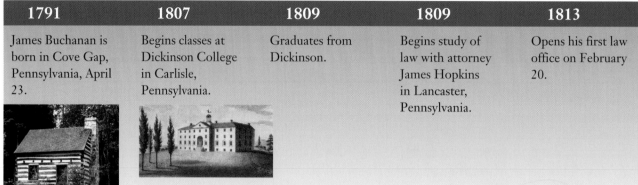

1791	1807	1809	1809	1813
James Buchanan is born in Cove Gap, Pennsylvania, April 23.	Begins classes at Dickinson College in Carlisle, Pennsylvania.	Graduates from Dickinson.	Begins study of law with attorney James Hopkins in Lancaster, Pennsylvania.	Opens his first law office on February 20.

1845	1846	1848	1849	1853
President James K. Polk appoints Buchanan secretary of state.	Buchanan helps negotiate treaty bringing the Oregon Territory under U.S. control.	Consults on Treaty of Guadalupe Hidalgo, ending the U.S.-Mexican War.	Retires to Wheatland, his estate near Lancaster, Pennsylvania.	President Franklin Pierce appoints Buchanan minister to England.

1861	1861	1861	1865	1866
Mississippi, Florida, Alabama, Georgia, Louisiana, and Texas secede, January. Buchanan signs Kansas statehood bill, January 29.	Lincoln is inaugurated president, March 4. Buchanan returns to Wheatland.	Confederates fire on Fort Sumter, April 12. Civil War begins.	Confederacy surrenders, ending the Civil War.	Buchanan publishes *Mr. Buchanan's Administration on the Eve of Rebellion.* Harriet Lane marries Henry E. Johnston.

1814	1819	1820	1831	1833

Serves briefly in the Lancaster County Dragoons. Wins election to the Pennsylvania General Assembly and serves two terms.

Becomes engaged to Ann Coleman in July; she dies in December.

Elected to the U.S. House of Representatives; serves ten years.

Appointed minister to Russia, spends a year in St. Petersburg.

Returns to the United States; wins election to the U.S. Senate, serves 11 years.

1856	1857	1858	1859	1860

Buchanan is nominated for president June 2 and elected November 4.

Is inaugurated as 15th president, March 4. Dred Scott decision is handed down, March 6. New York Stock Exchange collapses August 24, beginning the Panic of 1857.

Treaties with China, Japan completed; controversy over Kansas continues.

John Brown raids Harper's Ferry arsenal, October 16. He is captured and convicted and is executed December 2.

Abraham Lincoln is elected president; South Carolina secedes, December 20; Major Robert Anderson occupies Fort Sumter, December 26.

1868

James Buchanan dies, June 1; is buried in Lancaster.

Glossary

abolitionist: in U.S. history, a person who believes that slavery should be ended, or abolished, immediately

annex: to make an outlying region part of a country's territory; the United States annexed Texas in 1845

arsenal: a government building or complex where arms and ammunition are stored

ballot: at a political convention, one round of voting to determine a party's candidate for a coming election; if no person receives the required number of votes, further ballots are taken until a winner is determined

caucus: in U.S. politics, a meeting of leaders of a political party to nominate a candidate for a coming election

impeach: in United States history, to charge a public official of serious crimes and try him or her; if found guilty, the official is removed from office

impress: in naval history, to capture a seaman and force him to serve on an enemy's ship

secede: to withdraw from a government; in 1860 and 1861, southern states seceded from the Union (the United States)

secretary of state: in U.S. government, the official appointed by the president to manage diplomacy and relations with other countries

Further Reading

Barber, James. *Eyewitness: Presidents*. New York: DK Publishing, 2000.

Bausum, Ann. *Our Country's Presidents*. Washington DC: National Geographic Society, 2001.

Blassingame, Wyatt. *Look-It-Up Book of Presidents*. New York: Random House, 1990.

Joseph, Paul. *James Buchanan*. Edina, MN: Abdo Publishers, 2001.

Pascoe, Elaine. *First Facts About the Presidents*. Woodbridge, CT: Blackbirch Publishing, 1996.

Santella, Andrew. *James Buchanan*. Minneapolis, MN: Compass Point Books, 2003.

Young, Jeff C. *James Buchanan*. Berkeley Heights, NJ: Enslow Publishers, 2003.

MORE ADVANCED READING

Binder, Frederick Moore. *James Buchanan and the American Empire*. Cranbury, NJ: Associated University Presses, 1994.

Birkner, Michael J., ed. *James Buchanan and the Political Crisis of the 1850s*. Cranbury, NJ: Associated University Presses, 1996.

Klein, Phillip Shriver. *President James Buchanan, A Biography*. University Park: Pennsylvania State University Press, 1962.

Places to Visit

★ ★ ★ ★ ★

Wheatland Historic Site

1120 Marietta Avenue

Lancaster, PA 17603

The estate of James Buchanan, which has been restored and displays memorabilia of Buchanan's life and presidency.

The White House

1600 Pennsylvania Avenue NW

Washington, DC 20500

Visitors' Office: (202) 456-7041

Buchanan lived in the White House from 1857 to 1861.

Buchanan's Birthplace State Park

c/o Cowans Gap State Park

6235 Aughwick Road

Fort Loudon, PA 17224

This park preserves part of the Cove Gap trading post operated by James Buchanan Senior, where his son, the future president, was born in 1791.

Online Sites of Interest

* **Internet Public Library, Presidents of the United States (IPL-POTUS)**

  http:/www.ipl.org/div/potus/jbuchanan.html

  This excellent site offers facts about James Buchanan and links to other sites of interest. The site is operated by the University of Michigan.

* **americanpresident.org**

  http://www.americanpresident.org/history/jamesbuchanan/

  An opening thumbnail biography is supported by pages with more detailed information on Buchanan's early life, political career, and presidency. The site is operated by the Miller Center at the University of Virginia.

* **The White House**

  http://www.whitehouse.gov/history/presidents/jb15.html

  Provides a brief biography of Buchanan. Other parts of the site offer information on the current president, and the history of the White House itself.

* **Wheatland Virtual Tour**

  http://www.pennmanor.net/wheatland/vt.html

  Provides an online tour of the house and biographical information on Buchanan and his niece Harriet Lane, who served as first lady during his presidency.

Table of Presidents

	1. George Washington	2. John Adams	3. Thomas Jefferson	4. James Madison
Took office	Apr 30 1789	Mar 4 1797	Mar 4 1801	Mar 4 1809
Left office	Mar 3 1797	Mar 3 1801	Mar 3 1809	Mar 3 1817
Birthplace	Westmoreland Co, VA	Braintree, MA	Shadwell, VA	Port Conway, VA
Birth date	Feb 22 1732	Oct 20 1735	Apr 13 1743	Mar 16 1751
Death date	Dec 14 1799	July 4 1826	July 4 1826	June 28 1836

	9. William H. Harrison	10. John Tyler	11. James K. Polk	12. Zachary Taylor
Took office	Mar 4 1841	Apr 6 1841	Mar 4 1845	Mar 5 1849
Left office	**Apr 4 1841•**	Mar 3 1845	Mar 3 1849	**July 9 1850•**
Birthplace	Berkeley, VA	Greenway, VA	Mecklenburg Co, NC	Barboursville, VA
Birth date	Feb 9 1773	Mar 29 1790	Nov 2 1795	Nov 24 1784
Death date	Apr 4 1841	Jan 18 1862	June 15 1849	July 9 1850

	17. Andrew Johnson	18. Ulysses S. Grant	19. Rutherford B. Hayes	20. James A. Garfield
Took office	Apr 15 1865	Mar 4 1869	Mar 5 1877	Mar 4 1881
Left office	Mar 3 1869	Mar 3 1877	Mar 3 1881	**Sept 19 1881•**
Birthplace	Raleigh, NC	Point Pleasant, OH	Delaware, OH	Orange, OH
Birth date	Dec 29 1808	Apr 27 1822	Oct 4 1822	Nov 19 1831
Death date	July 31 1875	July 23 1885	Jan 17 1893	Sept 19 1881

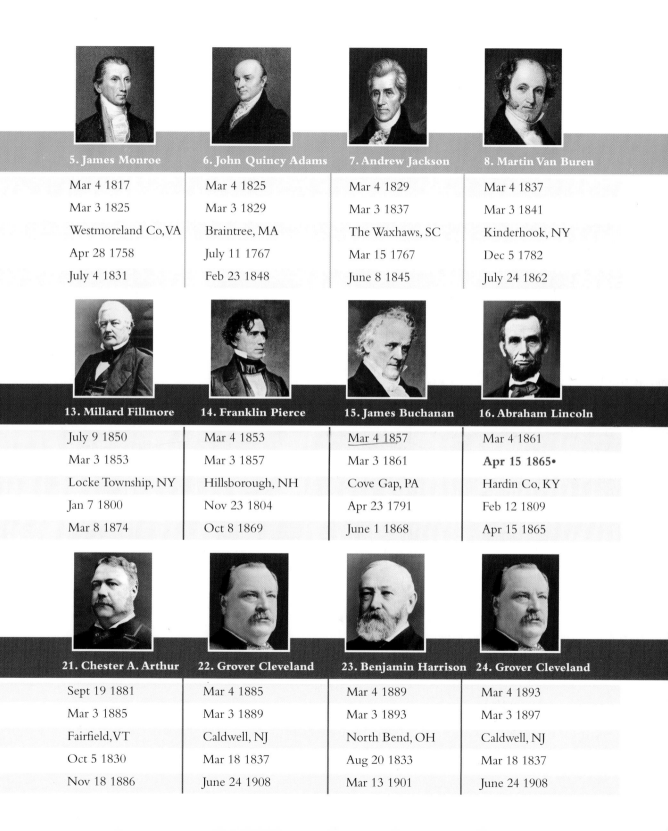

5. James Monroe	**6. John Quincy Adams**	**7. Andrew Jackson**	**8. Martin Van Buren**
Mar 4 1817	Mar 4 1825	Mar 4 1829	Mar 4 1837
Mar 3 1825	Mar 3 1829	Mar 3 1837	Mar 3 1841
Westmoreland Co, VA	Braintree, MA	The Waxhaws, SC	Kinderhook, NY
Apr 28 1758	July 11 1767	Mar 15 1767	Dec 5 1782
July 4 1831	Feb 23 1848	June 8 1845	July 24 1862

13. Millard Fillmore	**14. Franklin Pierce**	**15. James Buchanan**	**16. Abraham Lincoln**
July 9 1850	Mar 4 1853	Mar 4 1857	Mar 4 1861
Mar 3 1853	Mar 3 1857	Mar 3 1861	**Apr 15 1865•**
Locke Township, NY	Hillsborough, NH	Cove Gap, PA	Hardin Co, KY
Jan 7 1800	Nov 23 1804	Apr 23 1791	Feb 12 1809
Mar 8 1874	Oct 8 1869	June 1 1868	Apr 15 1865

21. Chester A. Arthur	**22. Grover Cleveland**	**23. Benjamin Harrison**	**24. Grover Cleveland**
Sept 19 1881	Mar 4 1885	Mar 4 1889	Mar 4 1893
Mar 3 1885	Mar 3 1889	Mar 3 1893	Mar 3 1897
Fairfield, VT	Caldwell, NJ	North Bend, OH	Caldwell, NJ
Oct 5 1830	Mar 18 1837	Aug 20 1833	Mar 18 1837
Nov 18 1886	June 24 1908	Mar 13 1901	June 24 1908

	25. William McKinley	26. Theodore Roosevelt	27. William H. Taft	28. Woodrow Wilson
Took office	Mar 4 1897	Sept 14 1901	Mar 4 1909	Mar 4 1913
Left office	Sept 14 1901•	Mar 3 1909	Mar 3 1913	Mar 3 1921
Birthplace	Niles, OH	New York, NY	Cincinnati, OH	Staunton, VA
Birth date	Jan 29 1843	Oct 27 1858	Sept 15 1857	Dec 28 1856
Death date	Sept 14 1901	Jan 6 1919	Mar 8 1930	Feb 3 1924

	33. Harry S. Truman	34. Dwight D. Eisenhower	35. John F. Kennedy	36. Lyndon B. Johnson
Took office	Apr 12 1945	Jan 20 1953	Jan 20 1961	Nov 22 1963
Left office	Jan 20 1953	Jan 20 1961	Nov 22 1963•	Jan 20 1969
Birthplace	Lamar, MO	Denison, TX	Brookline, MA	Johnson City, TX
Birth date	May 8 1884	Oct 14 1890	May 29 1917	Aug 27 1908
Death date	Dec 26 1972	Mar 28 1969	Nov 22 1963	Jan 22 1973

	41. George Bush	42. Bill Clinton	43. George W. Bush	
Took office	Jan 20 1989	Jan 20 1993	Jan 20 2001	
Left office	Jan 20 1993	Jan 20 2001	—	
Birthplace	Milton, MA	Hope, AR	New Haven, CT	
Birth date	June 12 1924	Aug 19 1946	July 6 1946	
Death date	—	—	—	

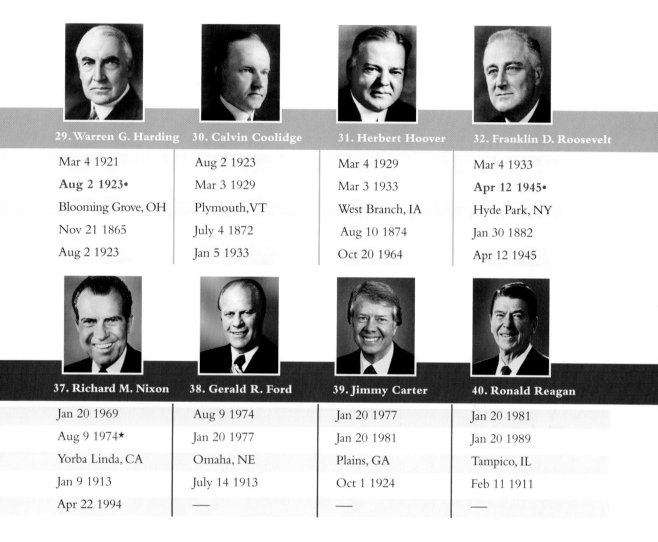

29. Warren G. Harding

Mar 4 1921

Aug 2 1923•

Blooming Grove, OH

Nov 21 1865

Aug 2 1923

30. Calvin Coolidge

Aug 2 1923

Mar 3 1929

Plymouth, VT

July 4 1872

Jan 5 1933

31. Herbert Hoover

Mar 4 1929

Mar 3 1933

West Branch, IA

Aug 10 1874

Oct 20 1964

32. Franklin D. Roosevelt

Mar 4 1933

Apr 12 1945•

Hyde Park, NY

Jan 30 1882

Apr 12 1945

37. Richard M. Nixon

Jan 20 1969

Aug 9 1974★

Yorba Linda, CA

Jan 9 1913

Apr 22 1994

38. Gerald R. Ford

Aug 9 1974

Jan 20 1977

Omaha, NE

July 14 1913

—

39. Jimmy Carter

Jan 20 1977

Jan 20 1981

Plains, GA

Oct 1 1924

—

40. Ronald Reagan

Jan 20 1981

Jan 20 1989

Tampico, IL

Feb 11 1911

—

• Indicates the president died while in office.

★ Richard Nixon resigned before his term expired.

Index

Page numbers in *italics* indicate illustrations.

About the Author

☆

Allison Lassieur has written more than 40 books about famous figures, history, world cultures, current events, science, and health. In addition to writing, Ms. Lassieur studies medieval textile history. She lives in Pennsylvania in a hundred-year-old house with her husband Chuck and their two cats, Ulysses and Oberon.